A PROPOSED UNITED STATES GRAND STRATEGY FOR 2015 – 2030

The global situation currently facing the United States in 2012 has evolved based upon qualified U.S. success in Iraq, the continued accomplishments of global efforts against extremist organizations, the on-going events of the "Arab Spring," the regime change in Libya, and the anticipated drawdown and withdrawal of U.S. forces from Afghanistan by 2014. Although sustained American and partner efforts are needed to both stabilize the situation in the Afghanistan-Pakistan region and contain the growing threat of Iranian power in the Middle East, the strategic opportunity is now present for the United States, given its weakened economic circumstances in both the present and projected over the next two decades, to thoughtfully reassess its future role and position in the international system. Richard Haass, President of the Council on Foreign Relations notes, "...21st-century international relations will be characterized by nonpolarity: a world dominated not by one, two or even several states but rather by dozens of states and other actors possessing and exercising military, economic, diplomatic and cultural power."[1] While still the most powerful country, the U.S. must recognize and acknowledge its decrease in power relative to the rise of other nations and actors, and adjust its national security and economic policies appropriately. Military theorist Liddell Hart made the following point, which properly reflects the current U.S. situation, in stating, "The experience of history brings ample evidence that the downfall of civilized states tends to come not from the direct assaults of foes but from internal decay, combined with the consequences of exhaustion in war."[2] Economist Fred Bergsten elaborates on this point in declaring, "...unless the United States quickly achieves and maintains a sustainable economic position, its ability to pursue autonomous economic and foreign policies will become increasingly compromised."[3]

The status quo of U.S. policy cannot hold; change is needed.

This reevaluation effort is necessary owing to the severe, long-term economic situation faced by the U.S., but this fact need not mean a wholesale American withdrawal from the international scene into isolationism or an abandonment of its core strategic objectives and interests. Strategic analyst Patrick Cronin asserts,

> American leadership in the world remains essential, positive and coveted by our allies, but our top priority must be to realign our ambitions and our resources to build a solid foundation for the future. America's long-term influence is being eroded by having to spend an ever-larger percentage of its capital and legitimacy managing short-term financial and military crises. If the United States fails to get its economic house in order, by the end of this decade it may well be carrying a federal debt close to 100 percent of GDP.[4]

The U.S. must recognize and adapt to the fact that it will no longer be the world's hegemon[5], but will operate for the foreseeable future in a world of nation-states rising at varying stages to regional and global power. Haass further observes, "Power will increasingly be found in many hands and many places. The result will be a world where power diffuses, not concentrates."[6] CNN Foreign Policy Commentator Fareed Zakaria goes as far to declare that the U.S. is moving into a post-American world, "...one defined and directed from many places and by many people."[7] This nation must therefore integrate two fundamental undercurrents of thought during this reassessment: first, the U.S. aspires to remain an uniquely important player on the international scene, but as Professors Paul MacDonald and Joseph Parent point out, "If declining states mismatch their foreign policy means and ends for a significant length of time, they will hemorrhage resources and be contemptible competitors in the game of great power politics;"[8] and secondly, this country must develop an appropriate grand strategy to answer what has been an identifiable pattern of questions throughout history for a declining hegemon as Professor Steven Lobell asks, "Who to punish, where to cooperate, and how to allocate national resources between its productive capacity and military security?"[9] These considerations form the larger, conceptual foundation for grand strategy development.

This paper examines the need for the development of a comprehensive U.S. grand strategy for the period 2015 to 2030 to secure the nation's place within the emerging international system. The U.S. must modify its current national security plans and policies in order to accomplish a successful regeneration of its national capabilities during this timeframe. The primary premise of this paper is that for the U.S. to preserve its ability to function as a great power within the international system of the 2030 to 2040 timeframe, this country must regenerate its economic strength and recapitalize select defense capabilities during the 2015 to 2030 period. Not doing so risks this nation's long-term global position and power into the mid-21st century. This examination includes a review of current U.S. national security objectives and the future operating environment, provides analysis of the current U.S. economic situation and its impact on future grand strategy, includes a historical review of selected, past great powers and their efforts to maintain power within the international system, and offers recommendations for designing a U.S. grand strategy for the 2015 to 2030 timeframe.

Hegemon and Grand Strategy

Lobell clearly states in such an endeavor, the goal for a former hegemon, or one in relative decline, is to, "…balance capabilities and global commitments without eroding its economic staying power."[10] In the U.S. case, the goal is to rebuild its already eroded and weakened economic foundations. Lobell additionally states, "In shifting from a

3

hegemonic to a multi-polar distribution of power, the grand strategy of a declining state is to remain in the ranks of the great powers as long as possible. As a great power, the former hegemon can preserve the existing international order, which is compatible with its commercial and security interests."[11] This ambition is consistent with current U.S. policy. The nation must realign and balance its objectives and goals over the next 15 years to regenerate its economic capacity and consequently retain global power and influence in the decade to come, so that the U.S. can preserve its place within the existing international system.

Given these larger aims and purposes, how is grand strategy expressed or defined as means to clearly establish the parameters under which this paper uses the term? No formal or common definition exists, and various authors have offered their own definitions to fill this void. Professor Robert Art plainly states, "The goal of grand strategy should be to keep the latent threats latent and to remove, or if not possible, then lessen, those that have become more manifest."[12] Professor John Mearsheimer, chronicler of Liddell Hart, offers a strictly military-oriented characterization for his analysis when he proclaims that grand strategy consists of two important questions, "First, what are the principal military threats from abroad and how should they be ordered? In other words, how should a state rank-order its overseas defense commitments? Second, what kinds of military forces should a state develop to support these commitments"[13] Mearsheimer states that grand strategy can actually include the larger process of integrating a nation's diplomatic and economic capabilities with its military power,[14] which is evidenced by Liddell Hart's own definition when he explains that grand strategy means, "to coordinate and direct all the resources of the nation, or band of nations, towards the attainment of the political objective of the war – the goal defined by fundamental policy…[it] looks beyond the war to the subsequent peace."[15] Professor Wiliamson Murray also takes a broader view of grand strategy's purpose during both wartime and peace in declaring,

> ….grand strategy is more often than not about the ability to adjust to the reality that resources, will, and interests inevitably find themselves out of balance in some areas……it is about insuring that the balance is right in those areas that matter most….It demands a recognition of and ability to react to the ever-shifting environments of war and peace……those who develop a successful grand strategy never lose sight of the long-term goal, whatever that might be, but are willing to adapt to the difficulties of the present in reaching toward the future. Grand Strategy lies at the nexus of politics and military strategy and thus contains important elements of both…it exists in a world of constant flux, one in which uncertainty and ambiguity dominate.[16]

On the other hand, Professor Daniel Drezner offers a somewhat contrarian view asserting that judgment about a nation's actions and its power is far more important than its stated grand strategy, but also says, "Still, in times of deep uncertainty, a strategy can be important as a signaling device. In these moments, such as the present, a clearly articulated strategy matched by consistent actions is useful because it can drive home messages about a country's intentions to domestic and foreign audiences."[17] In the spirit of declaring those intentions, and encompassing a view that all elements of national power are consequential and require synchronization, this author defines *Grand Strategy* as, "A conceptual blueprint that describes how a nation will plan, employ, and manage its elements of national power and capabilities towards the attainment of its national security goals and guarantee its desired place within the international system of nation-states." Drezner adds that grand strategies really do count and that, "Ideas matter most when actors are operating in unchartered waters. They can function as cognitive beacons, guiding countries to safety."[18]

Future Environment

Given the need for a grand strategy and given this established definition to assist in illuminating that beacon, what international environment of the 2015 to 2030 timeframe and beyond confronts the U.S.? Murray further offers, "At present, Americans confront the most confusing and uncertain strategic environment in their history...The problem for Americans in thinking about the issues in a grand strategy's development and execution is that there are no easy, simple solutions; there are no silver bullets,"[19] and in contrast to Cronin, Professor Robert Art declares, "The future is not likely to be so rosy for the United States. Other states, including America's allies, are growing restive of America's predominant position and are all likely to challenge it."[20] U.S. leaders must recognize the world is rapidly changing and the U.S. strategic position within that world is shifting, and they must appreciate the implications for the nation's future place in the international system. More specifically, the National Intelligence Council (NIC) offers the following analysis,

> The *international system*—as constructed following the Second World War—will be almost unrecognizable by 2025 owing to the rise of emerging powers, a globalizing economy, a historic transfer of relative wealth and economic power from West to East, and the growing influence of non-state actors. By 2025, the international system will be a *global multipolar one* with gaps in national power continuing to narrow between developed and developing countries...Concurrent with the shift in power among nation-states, the relative power of various non-state actors—including businesses, tribes, religious organizations, and criminal networks—is increasing. Historically, emerging multipolar systems have been more unstable than bipolar or unipolar ones.[21]

In 2010, United States Joint Forces Command (USJFCOM) offered this assessment which further reinforces the challenging nature of the future international environment,

> In thinking about the world's trajectory, we have reason to believe that the next 25 years will bring changes just as dramatic, drastic, and disruptive as those that have occurred in the past quarter century...the pace of

technological and scientific change is increasing. Changes will occur throughout the energy, financial, political, strategic, operational, and technological domains. How drastic, how disruptive and how surprising these changes might be is at present not discernible and in some cases their full impact will not be understood until they are upon us.[22]

Although the NIC concludes the U.S. will remain the world's most powerful actor, the relative decline in its strength means more constraints in the use of national power, coupled with increased global risks during the transition to this new system or in dealing with disruptive changes. The NIC states, "Strategic rivalries are most likely to revolve around trade, investments, and technological innovation and acquisition, but we cannot rule out a 19th century-like scenario of arms races, territorial expansion, and military rivalries."[23] The U.S. must prepare now for that future as global transformations and international system challenges facing the nation generally fall into four overlapping categories: rising powers and economic standing, the U.S. fiscal posture, technological innovations, and the changing nature of conflict. First, the economic rise of the so-called BRIC nations (Brazil, Russia, India and China) constitutes multiple challenges to the U.S. across economic, military, and global power domains.

> In terms of size, speed, and directional flow, the transfer of [relative] *global wealth and economic power* now under way—roughly from West to East— is without precedent in modern history. This shift derives from two sources. First, increases in oil and commodity prices have generated windfall profits for the Gulf states and Russia. Second, lower costs combined with government policies have shifted the locus of manufacturing and some service industries to Asia. Growth projections for Brazil, Russia, India, and China...indicate they will collectively match the original G-7's share of global GDP by 2040-2050.[24]

Relative U.S. economic power has trended downward since the Cold War's end and its share of global GDP has declined, while that of the BRIC nations has increased. By 2014, BRIC countries will represent more than 27 percent of global GDP, while the U.S. and the European Union will represent less than 20 percent each, according to

International Monetary Fund (IMF) estimates.[25]

The emergence of China has caused the most strategic concern within the international system, and no other single country is poised to have more impact on the world over the next 20 years. If current trends persist, by 2025 China will maintain the world's second largest economy, both in nominal and purchasing power parity (PPP) terms, and will be a leading military power.[26] Senior fellow at the Center for Global Development Arvind Subramanian takes a far harsher view in stating by 2030, "…relative U.S. decline will have yielded not a multipolar world but a near-unipolar one dominated by China." He argues China will lead the world in both trade and GDP at that time and "China's future economic dominance is more imminent and will be both greater and more varied than is currently supposed."[27] On the other hand, Harvard research fellow Michael Beckley calls Subramanian's estimation of Chinese power over-inflated and defined by narrow parameters, concluding that long-term trends point to a continued U.S. lead over China in economic, technological, and military terms.[28] Reflecting this author's view, Richard Haass basically splits the difference, reinforcing the notion that U.S. power has changed relative to these nations; he sees both Chinese and other rising powers' motivations as evolutionary, not revolutionary, thus seeking to integrate into and only partially change the existing international order.[29]

The debate will continue to rage as to the degree that China's rise, and those of other rising nations, will impact U.S. power into the future. Adding to the complexity of dealing with this on-going issue and certainly less debatable, the second future challenge facing the U.S. is its own fiscal and economic situation. The Great Recession of 2008 had a severe effect and it "accelerated the trends that are shifting the world's center of gravity away from the United States...US losses in home-equity savings, retirement accounts, pension assets...totaled 8.3 trillion dollars." In addition, China was not impacted by this event and it gave "China the opportunity to solidify its strategic advantages as the U.S. and Europe struggle to recover..."[30] In terms of the U.S. fiscal posture, the Congressional Budget Office (CBO) projects,

> ...persistent U.S. budget deficits for the next 25 years—even under its optimistic "baseline" scenario—and it warns of plausible alternatives in which total federal debt would exceed 100 percent of GDP by 2023 and 190 percent of GDP by 2035. State and local governments are hurting too, which means less money for roads, bridges, schools, law enforcement and the other collective goods that help maintain a healthy society...The financial meltdown also undermined an important element of America's "soft power," namely, its reputation for competence and probity in economic policy.[31]

The U.S. fiscal situation could negatively impact our currency and the advantage it currently gives the nation within the international finance system as the NIC points out,

> The dollar is vulnerable to a major financial crisis and the dollar's international role is likely to decline from that of the unparalleled "global reserve currency," to something of a first among equals in a basket of currencies by 2025.....While total loss of reserve status is unlikely, the dollar's decline may force the US into difficult tradeoffs between achieving ambitious foreign policy goals and the high domestic costs of supporting those objectives. In the face of higher interest rates, higher taxes, and potential oil shocks, the US public would have to weigh the economic consequences of taking strong military action...In addition, US financial dependence on external powers for fiscal stability may curtail US freedom of action in unanticipated ways.[32]

The U.S. faces the real possibility of not having sufficient resources or economic strength to execute the totality of its future national security requirements. This paper will examine in greater detail the U.S. economic situation and its national security implications in a subsequent section.

Thus, the need to husband resources and re-establish a firm economic foundation to face those rising powers is heightened by the third major challenge of the future, that of being able to leverage and exploit technological change and innovation to the nation's benefit. The U.S. must position itself with sufficient fiscal resources over the next 15 years to innovate and utilize technology from across multiple emerging fields, many of which have the potential to bring both economic advantage and military value in maintaining U.S. great power status into the 2030 – 2040 timeframe. Some of the more promising technologies are listed in the table below:

Emerging Technology	Description
Clean Water	Comprises a range of technologies that enable faster and more energy efficient treatment of fresh water and waste water, and desalination of brackish and sea water, to provide sustainable and diverse water sources.
Ubiquitous Computing	Will be enabled by widespread tagging and networking of mundane objects such as food packages, furniture, room sensors, and paper documents.
Energy Storage	Encompasses a wide range of materials and techniques for storing energy, a necessity for the viability of many alternatives to fossil-fuel energy sources.
Biogeron	The science related to the study of the cellular and molecular basis of disease and aging applied to the development of new technological means for identifying and treating diseases and disabilities associated with old age.
Clean Coal	Includes various combinations of carbon capture sequestration (CCS) to prohibit CO_2—a byproduct of burning coal—from entering the atmosphere; coal conversion into syngas (gasification); and processes to convert syngas to hydrocarbons.
Human Strength Augmentation	Involves mechanical and electronic systems that supplement human physical capabilities.
Biofuels	Used to produce ethanol from crops such as corn and sugarcane and biodiesel from crops such as grapeseed and soy. Next-generation processes will convert lignocellulosic materials to fuels. Significant potential also exists to cultivate high-growth microalgae for conversion to biodiesel and other biofuels.
Service Robotics	Comprise robots and unmanned vehicles for non-manufacturing applications, using a large number of enabling technologies including hardware (e.g. sensors, actuators, power systems) and software platforms (advanced systems might incorporate behavioral algorithms and artificial intelligence). These technologies would enable a wide variety of remote controlled, semiautonomous (with human intervention), and completely autonomous robotic systems.
Human Cognitive Augmentation	Includes drugs, implants, virtual learning environments, and wearable devices to enhance human cognitive abilities.

Table 1 – Emerging Technologies 2020 to 2030[33]

Additionally, fossil-based fuels will remain the foundation of global energy requirements, but the NIC states, "Despite what are seen as long odds now, we cannot rule out the possibility of an energy transition by 2025 that would avoid the costs of an energy infrastructure overhaul. The greatest possibility for a relatively quick and inexpensive transition during the period comes from better renewable generation sources (photovoltaic and wind) and improvements in battery technology."[34] Without structural improvements to enhance the nation's economic competitiveness during the next decade, the U.S. risks falling behind other powers in its ability to exploit emerging technologies to sustain its economic power. The 2010 JOE concludes, "It is by no means certain that the United States and its allies will maintain their overall lead in *technological* development over the next 25 years…any militarily-significant technological surprise is likely to result from the combination of one or more technologies, and the novel use of the resulting combinations.[35]

These technological surprises could negatively magnify the last area of future challenge, that of the changing character of conflict where modern information systems and enhanced denial and deception capabilities, allow potential adversaries, both state and non-state, to rapidly employ precision weaponry to devastating effect . Author Neyla Arnas points out that nation-states will "…remain dominant actors, but there is increasing influence of individuals, groups, the private sector and Non-Governmental Organizations upon the international system," and the international system will see increased proliferation of technologies and knowledge capabilities impacting future conflicts.[36] The NIC further elaborates in stating, "Conflict will continue to evolve over the next 20 years as potential combatants adapt to advances in science and technology, improving weapon capabilities, and changes in the security environment."[37]

Three specific trends are emerging that the U.S. must adapt to and prepare for in dealing with this future environment of conflict: first, the increasing importance of information capabilities that enable "new warfighting synergies through combinations of advanced precision weaponry, improving target and surveillance capabilities, enhanced command and control, and the expanding use of artificial intelligence and robotics;" secondly, the "Non-military means of warfare, such as... economic, resource, psychological, and information-based forms of conflict will become more prevalent...states and nonstate adversaries will engage in 'media warfare' to dominate the 24-hour news cycle and manipulate public opinion;" and lastly, "The advancement of weapons capabilities such as long-range precision weapons, WMD, and the employment of...cyber and space warfare are providing state militaries and nonstate groups the means to escalate and expand future conflicts beyond the traditional battlefield."[38] USJFCOM also clearly highlights the future cyber domain as particularly dangerous to U.S. national security in stating,

> Cyberspace permeates nearly every aspect of societies from personal computers and cell phones to networked transportation and inventory systems. Our society's very way of life has come to depend fundamentally on the use of cyberspace...Our ability to maneuver freely in cyberspace amplifies all instruments of national power. In fact, our ability to maneuver in cyberspace is an emerging instrument of power itself. Many of those same advances also will be available to America's opponents, who will use them to attack, degrade, and disrupt communications and the flow of information...Cyberspace represents an avenue of great national opportunity, but is also a major source of critical strategic challenges. Low barriers to entry coupled with the anonymous nature of activities in cyberspace greatly broaden the list of potential adversaries.[39]

The U.S. is facing a very menacing future environment as evidenced alone by the challenges in cyberspace, and the NIC provides an overall conclusion in asserting,

"The trend toward greater diffusion of authority and power...is likely to accelerate because of the emergence of new global players, the worsening institutional deficit, potential expansion of regional blocs, and enhanced strength of nonstate actors and networks."[40]

Current United States Policy

The U.S. must address its present shortcomings to prepare for this future and remain a great power. Given the future environment and the need for a comprehensive grand strategy for the 2015 to 2030 timeframe, what is the current state of U.S. strategic policy? Many consider the 2010 National Security Strategy, and its forerunners, to be the nation's "grand strategy." In over 50 pages of text, this document describes what the nation wants to achieve within the international system, to include advancing its four primary, enduring interests or national objectives:

- *Security*: The security of the U.S., its citizens, and U.S. allies and partners

- *Prosperity*: A strong, innovative, and growing U.S. economy in an open international economic system that promotes opportunity and prosperity

- *Values*: Respect for universal values at home and around the world

- *International Order*: An international order advanced by U.S. leadership that promotes peace, security, and opportunity through stronger cooperation to meet global challenges [41]

On closer examination, however, the document functions primarily as a copiously worded "shopping list" of desired goals that includes 18 subordinate aims or purposes and 81 separate initiatives that are not tied to available resources, not prioritized at the national level, and are not bound to any type of significant time horizon for achievement.

In reading this document one cannot ascertain whether "Promoting Food Security," addressing "Arctic Interests," "Reducing the Deficit," or "Preventing Attacks on and in the Homeland" have the higher priority for planning, resourcing, and execution. In many aspects, this strategy document continues the trend of global U.S. involvement that has been the norm since the end of World War II, and if pursued to its logical conclusion, will certainly bankrupt the nation. Author Michael Mandelbaum points out that from 1941 to 1991, the U.S. played the role of "Global Doctor" doing what was necessary to save the patient, and since the Cold War's end it has played the role of "Global Philanthropist" investing in worthy causes around the world.[42] In contrast, Cronin describes the U.S. as having a split national security personality: first as "Global Enforcer," pursuing a long-standing conviction of most of the American body politic that the U.S. must serve as global policeman and smotherer of all threats; and secondly as "Global Savior," driven by a strong idealistic impulse engrained into the American psyche that manifests itself in laudable desires to help develop weak states and guarantee human rights.[43] Cronin sums up the consequences of these personalities, "Driven by a realist impulse to be the global enforcer and a moral imperative to act as global savior, the United States remains disproportionately invested in managing international security relative to its limited resources."[44]

The current U.S. "grand strategic" plan, as represented by the nation's capstone national security strategy, falls necessarily short as a comprehensive concept and prioritized design of actions for the next 15 years that also meets the definition of "grand strategy" earlier in this paper. Retired U.S. Army Lieutenant General David Barno asserts,

14

....the United States should continue to pursue the ends of its longstanding global engagement strategy, but should do so using different ways and means than those codified in the Obama administration's current national security plans. A new version of America's global engagement strategy remains affordable, even in today's fiscal environment, and pursuing it will help prevent and deter conflicts in the years ahead.[45]

Art adds, "The most fundamental task in devising a grand strategy is to determine a state's national interests."[46] This process includes determining a prioritization of those strategic objectives and Art recommends classifying a state's national interests in three tiers: first, "Vital" interests are essential objectives that if not achieved will bring costs that are catastrophic to the nation or nearly so; second, interests that are "Highly Important," if achieved, bring great benefits to the state, and if denied, carry severe costs but are not catastrophic; and third, interests that are "Important" increases a nation's economic well-being, perhaps its security, and contributes to making the international environment more congenial to the state's interests, but whose potential value or loss is moderate not great.[47] Art's prioritization scheme serves as a useful approach for aligning national objectives within a grand strategy, and if properly applied, would demonstrate U.S. strategic competence and responsiveness. As MacDonald and Parent observe,

> Great powers that do not react with agility and alacrity to a lower position are unlikely to last in the unforgiving game of power politics. Rivals will be quick to detect and exploit incompetence...States, like firms, tend to go bankrupt when they budget blithely and live beyond their means.[48]

Current Economic Situation

Given the present status of US "grand strategic" planning, what is even more troubling is the current condition of the nation's economic capabilities and resources; this situation is mainly the result of budgeting "blithely" and living "beyond our means," and negatively impacts the nation's long-term, great power status. The importance of economic strength is not lost on one of our main allies, as the Honorable Liam Fox, British Secretary of State for Defence, observes,

> The lessons of history are clear. Relative economic power is the wellspring of strategic strength. And conversely, economic weakness debilitates every arm of government. Structural economic weakness, if not dealt with, will bring an unavoidable reduction in our ability to shape the world.[49]

Primary emphasis for this paper, therefore, is focused on U.S. economic competitiveness, which is the main overall driver of economic growth. The World Economic Forum (WEF) delivers an annual report that ranks national economies by their relative competitiveness which the WEF defines,

> ...as the set of institutions, policies, and factors that determines the level of productivity of a country. The level of productivity, in turn, sets the sustainable level of prosperity that can be earned by an economy...more competitive economies tend to be able to produce higher levels of income for their citizens. The productivity level also determines the rates of return obtained by investments (physical, human, and technological) in an economy. Because the rates of return are the fundamental drivers of the growth rates of the economy, a more competitive economy is one that is likely to grow faster in the medium to long run.[50]

For the 2010 – 2011 timeframe the WEF notes, "The United States continues the decline that began last year, falling two more places to 4th position. While many structural features that make its economy extremely productive, a number of escalating weaknesses have lowered the US ranking over the past two years."[51]

The WEF basis its analysis on twelve pillars of competiveness, grouped into three major categories.[52] The U.S. ranks 3rd overall in the intermediate category of "Efficiency Enhancers" that contains six pillars, while it ranks 4th globally in the highest category of "Innovation and Sophistication Factors" that contains two pillars.[53] Its position is respectable for now in these two categories, but continued success into the future rests on a solid foundation. The U.S. possesses serious uncertainties with regards to its economic fundamentals, on the other hand, as the WEF ranked the U.S. 32nd globally in the "Basic Requirements" category which consists of 4 essential pillars.[54] The first of these pillars is "Institutional Environment" which the WEF states,

> ...is determined by the legal and administrative framework within which individuals, firms, and governments interact to generate income and wealth...The quality of institutions has a strong bearing on competitiveness and growth. It influences investment decisions and the organization of production and plays a key role in the ways in which societies distribute the benefits and bear the costs of development strategies and policies...[55]

The U.S. ranked 40th in this pillar and its implications have already appeared. The NIC observes about U.S. economic competitors,

> A generation of globally competitive companies is emerging from the new powers, helping to further solidify their position in the global marketplace; from Brazil in agribusiness and offshore energy exploration; Russia in energy and metals; India in IT services, pharmaceuticals, and auto parts; and China in steel, home appliances, and telecommunications equipment. Of the top 100 new global corporate leaders from the non-OECD world listed in a 2006 report from The Boston Consulting Group, 84 were headquartered in Brazil, Russia, China and India.[56]

As another measure, the annual U.S. growth of public and private research and development (R&D) spending in the past decade has been 3 to 5%, which is down from a long-term historic growth rate of 6 to 8%, and the U.S. share of global R&D funding continues to drop while China's share continues to grow (in 2012, the U.S. global share went from 32.8% to 31.1%).[57]

The second of the basic pillars is "Infrastructure" with the U.S. ranked 15th globally. The WEF observes that,

> Extensive and efficient infrastructure is critical for ensuring the effective functioning of the economy, as it is an important factor determining the location of economic activity and the kinds of activities or sectors that can develop in a particular economy...In addition, the quality and

extensiveness of infrastructure networks significantly impact economic growth...[58]

The condition of this nation's overall infrastructure is declining rapidly, given an overall grade of "D" by the American Society of Civil Engineers (ASCE) in their 2009 report. As the oldest engineering society in the U.S., ASCE gives an individual letter ranking to 15 subordinate infrastructure categories in order to arrive at the overall grade. The report asserts that: 26% of the nation's bridges are either structurally deficient or functionally obsolete; 33% of America's major roads are in poor or mediocre condition and current spending of $70.3 billion per year for highway capital improvements is well below the estimated $186 billion needed annually to substantially improve conditions; drinking water systems face an annual shortfall of at least $11 billion to replace aging facilities that are near the end of their useful life and to comply with existing and future federal water regulations; replacement cost to the aging locks of our inland waterway system is estimated at more than $125 billion despite the economic savings waterways can offer, and little has been done to improve their condition since 2005; more than $200 billion is needed through 2035 to accommodate anticipated growth in economically-efficient rail traffic; and the nation requires a projected $1.5 trillion in electric system investment through 2030 to keep up with growing demand coupled with maintenance and grid upgrade. Overall, there exists a national capital spending shortfall for the next five years of $1.18 trillion to repair and invest in the nation's infrastructure.[59] Currently the U.S. spends less than 2% of its Gross Domestic Product (GDP) on infrastructure while China and India are spending 9% and 5%, respectively.[60] Although greater nominally, the U.S. is spending less than required to sustain its economic foundations even in the short-term. Noted industrialist and former CEO of Loral Space & Communications,

Bernard Schwartz concludes, "...if we want to keep America as a first-tier nation for our children and grand-children, we must increase our infrastructure investment."[61]

The third basic pillar is the human capital-oriented "Health and Primary Education," and the WEF ranks the U.S. a paltry 42nd globally. The WEF describes the importance of this area in stating,

> A healthy workforce is vital to a country's competitiveness and productivity. Workers who are ill cannot function to their potential and will be less productive. Poor health leads to significant costs to business, as sick workers are often absent or operate at lower levels of efficiency... Basic education increases the efficiency of each individual worker. Moreover, workers who have received little formal education can carry out only simple manual work and find it much more difficult to adapt to more advanced production processes and techniques. Lack of basic education can therefore become a constraint on business development, with firms finding it difficult to move up the value chain by producing more sophisticated or value-intensive products.[62]

Investment in U.S. human capital capabilities is a fundamental precursor to sustained economic productivity and growth, not to mention the foundation of a well-educated and healthy military recruit pool. It also lays the groundwork for creative thinking, language proficiency and communication skills, all enablers for interaction with economic competitors and partners alike to the nation's benefit. Professor Sean Kay states, "In an era of global security, states that cultivate a citizenry that can work effectively with people across borders are likely to gain significant strategic advantage."[63]

The fourth and last basic pillar represents the most serious weakness to U.S. economic competitiveness now and into the future, that of its "Macroeconomic Environment" which is ranked a dismal 87th world-wide. The WEF states,

> The stability of the macroeconomic environment is important for business and, therefore, is important for the overall competitiveness of a country... macroeconomic disarray harms the economy. The government cannot provide services efficiently if it has to make high-interest payments on its past debts. Running fiscal deficits limits the government's future ability to

react to business cycles. Firms cannot operate efficiently when inflation rates are out of hand. In sum, the economy cannot grow in a sustainable manner unless the macroeconomic environment is stable.[64]

The U.S. economic and fiscal situation is dire reflecting increasing deficit and debt levels, increasing government expenditures on entitlement programs, declining defense spending relative to GDP, and slow economic growth. The list of economic and fiscal problems that the U.S. must solve are extremely daunting:

- In 2011, U.S. federal government debt was last reported at 93.2% of the nation's GDP. From 1940 to 2010, the average federal debt to GDP ratio was 59.4%. In 2010 alone, the U.S. government budget deficit was equivalent to 10.3% of GDP.[65] In that same year, federal government spending rose to 24% of GDP, 5 to 6% higher than its post-Cold War average.[66]

- The U.S. share of global GDP has dropped dropped from 23% in 1999 to 20% in 2009 while U.S. debt as a percentage of GDP doubled from 2001 to 2009, which does not count state and local government debt.[67]

- US Deficit was $1.3 trillion in 2008 and projected to be $1 trillion annually through 2020. By 2030, the United States could very well be transferring 7% of its entire annual GDP to the rest of the world because the annual cost of servicing the debt will rise to $2.5 trillion, and this will lead to a long-term erosion of US living standards.[68]

- The Congressional Budget Office (CBO) estimates that mandatory entitlement spending on Medicare, Medicaid, Social Security, and other like programs will demand 12.7% of GDP in 2021, up from 10.3% in 2010. From 1971 to 2010, the average was 9.9%.[69] Spending on these entitlement programs, plus interest on the national debt, was projected in 2007 to be 67% of the federal budget by 2015, up from 59% in 2006.[70] The government's FY2012 Budget submission itself projected that mandatory entitlement spending plus interest payments in FY2014 would actually be 69% of the federal budget, totaling $2.749 trillion.[71]

- Defense spending as percentage of the federal budget continues to decline. During the Korean war it was 70%, during the Vietnam War its 50%, and during the Iraqi and Afghanistan Wars in 2007 it was 20%.[72] Current administration budget plans have U.S. defense spending declining to 15.6% of the budget and 3.6% of GDP by 2015.[73] Although this returns defense spending to Post-Cold War and pre-9/11 levels as a percentage of GDP, the question remains - what will this level of spending resource in terms of required military capabilities?

- U.S. GDP only expanded 1.50 percent in the third quarter of 2011but historically, from 1948 until 2010 US average annual GDP Growth was 3.25 percent.[74] U.S. annual GDP growth has been anemic since 2001 with the following percentages from 2006 through 2010, respectively (2.7, 1.9, 0, -3.5, 3.0), according to the World Bank.[75]

- The government's FY2012 Budget submission statistics, and the spending requests underlying them, relied upon an annual GDP growth rate of 5% and a corresponnding increase in tax revenues of 21%, far short of what the nation is currently achieving.[76] The government will thus plan to spend more in the future without the corresponding revenues to support those outlays; debt will therefore increase.

As early as 2006, the CBO concluded that deficits in coming years will not be due to recession, wars, or investments, but on spending more and more for the elderly and interest payments on accumulated debt.[77] David M. Walker, U.S. Comptroller General and CEO of the U.S. Government Accountability Office (GAO) from 1998 to 2008, founded the *Comeback America Initiative* (CAI) in 2010, an organization created to promote fiscal responsibility and sustainability to achieve solutions to America's fiscal imbalances. As part of that effort, CAI issued its *2011 Restoring Fiscal Sanity* Report which observed,

> Our nation's financial condition is worse than advertised. While today's around $1.4 trillion annual deficit and $14.3 trillion debt burden are a matter of great public concern, they do not represent the true threat to our future...The true threat is represented by the huge structural deficits and debt burdens that lie ahead if we do not change course...Over time, and without action, Social Security, Medicare, Medicaid, and other related social insurance program challenges will grow. Based on reasonable and sustainable assumptions, Social Security and Medicare alone are underfunded by approximately $46 trillion, according to the 2011 Social Security and Medicare Trustees' Report...When you combine our known liabilities with our unfunded obligations and various commitments and contingencies, the federal government was in an over $61 trillion financial hole, as of September 30, 2010. This amounts to about $200,000 per person and over $500,000 per household, and these amounts are increasing rapidly.[78]

Because the nation borrows so much to meet current spending needs and possesses these potentially enormous future unfunded requirements, the negative implications long-term to our economic well-being are apparent, but it also impacts execution of our national security policies. British Professor Iwan Morgan, from the London-based Institute for the Study of the Americas, asserts,

> America is like no other dominant power in modern history — because it depends on other countries for capital to sustain its military and economic dominance…Simply put, the world's pre-eminent military, geopolitical and economic power is also its largest debtor, which absorbs at least 80% of the savings that the rest of the world does not invest at [their] home.[79]

Commentator Fareed Zakaria acerbically adds, "Americans are borrowing 80% of the world's surplus savings and using it for consumption: they are selling off their assets to foreigners to buy a couple more lattes a day."[80] Author Niall Ferguson reinforces the larger point in stating, "…the United States has imperceptibly come to rely on East Asian capital to stabilize its unbalanced budgets. Many commentators have noted the very muted…reaction of China to recent American military interventions. Fewer have appreciated the extent to which China now helps underwrite American power."[81]

Ambassador Robert Hormats therefore adds, "A heavily debt-laden, over-obligated, revenue-squeezed government, highly dependent on foreign capital, creates major security vulnerabilities."[82] This fact is manifest in that dependence on foreign capital and creditors makes the U.S. susceptible to the leverage and desires of other great powers through potential deterrence or compellence. The U.S. could possibly be deterred from pursuing certain policies or compelled to act in certain ways actually detrimental to our interests because of our financial and economic vulnerabilities. A recent example of these possibilities should give pause as Professor Daniel Drezner points out in 2008 about U.S. government actions to head off a crisis in mortgage-lending institutions,

> ...the Treasury Department decided to put Fannie Mae and Freddie Mac into a government conservatorship. Foreign pressure for intervention clearly played a role in the decision. Senator Charles Schumer told the press that government officials informed him that "there was a real fear that foreign governments would start dumping Fannie and Freddie." Mark Zandiwrote immediately afterward that "it was the mounting evidence that central banks, sovereign wealth funds, and other global investors were growing reluctant to invest in the debt that was the catalyst for the Treasury Department'sactions.[83]

The Director of National Intelligence in 2008 declared, "...concerns about the financial capabilities of Russia, China, and OPEC countries and the potential use of market access to exert financial leverage to achieve political ends represents a major national security issue."[84] With regards to the U.S. situation, Ferguson cleverly reflects,

> ...[Paul] Kennedy's original thesis of *fiscal* overstretch might yet be vindicated....America's fiscal overstretch is far worse today than anything he envisaged sixteen years ago. The key point...is that this overstretch has almost nothing to do with the United States' overseas military commitments. It is the result of America's chronically unbalanced *domestic* finances....Americans like security. But they like Social Security more than national security.[85]

We must develop a long-term program to address our economic and financial situation in order to stabilize the nation's "Macroeconomic Environment" and its impact on U.S. economic competitiveness within the international system. As the WEF concludes,

> Prior to the crisis [of 2008], the United States had been building up large macroeconomic imbalances, with repeated fiscal deficits leading to burgeoning levels of public indebtedness; this has been exacerbated by significant stimulus spending. In this context it is clear that mapping out a clear exit strategy will be an important step in reinforcing the country's competitiveness going into the future.[86]

This exit strategy is imperative to avert financial demise or even collapse. Walker points out that the Western Roman Empire fell for many reasons, one being the fiscal irresponsibility of the central government.[87] Ferguson also suggests a possible U.S.

parallel to the Roman experience when he comments, "As Gibbon said, the finances of

a declining empire do indeed make an interesting subject."[88]

Lessons Known from the Past

Given the nation's current strategic posture, its future challenges, an incomplete

grand strategic design, and a sobering economic situation, what might the U.S. deduce

from the experiences of past hegemons' in some version of decline? Besides these

comparisons to ancient Rome, what lessons are not too late to discover and can be

applied to the nation's present quandaries? A specific lesson known for a nation's great

power status touched upon throughout this paper is the following: some government

debt is tolerable, more government debt is bad, and uncontrolled government debt is

nearly fatal. As the 2010 JOE highlights,

> Habsburg Spain defaulted on its debt some 14 times in 150 years and was
> staggered by high inflation until its overseas empire collapsed. Bourbon
> France became so beset by debt due to its many wars and extravagances
> that by 1788 the contributing social stresses resulted in its overthrow by
> revolution. Interest ate up 44% of the British Government budget during
> the interwar years 1919-1939, inhibiting its ability to rearm against a
> resurgent Germany. Unless current trends are reversed, the U.S. will face
> similar challenges, anticipating an ever-growing percentage of the U.S.
> government budget going to pay interest on the money borrowed to
> finance our deficit spending.[89]

Accumulated public debt functions as a "tax" on future generations' fiscal potential and a

"drag" on a nation's future economic growth, both the foundations of continued military

strength and great power status. Although not directly parallel to the current U.S.

situation, the experiences of previous hegemons, specifically Habsburg Spain and the

British Empire, offer useful insights for current American policy-makers. Former

Secretary of State Henry Kissinger comments, "Historical parallels are by nature inexact. And even the most precise analogy does not oblige the present generation to repeat the mistakes of its predecessors."[90]

Author Kevin Phillips points out that both empires, in addition to experiencing the debt problem, also underwent an economic transformation from an earlier emphasis on manufacturing and trade to that of high finance once the empire matured. Phillips explains,

> Through the prior centuries the most reliable signals of full-fledged or relative decline came when a leading power, its leaders over-confident from a generation or two at the center of world commerce, embraced global finance and services as the political economy of the future, allowing production or seafaring to fade...Developing a weakness in production or older forms of commerce—the Spanish wool industry...or British ironware—were recurring early symptoms, as were an emerging disproportion of financiers and rentiers coupled with an ever-increasing inclination to invest in government bonds or send money out of the country for a better return.[91]

The current U.S. economic and fiscal situation reflects some of these similar trends. Phillips further highlights the relationship of manufacturing, capital outflows, and relative decline in that Great Britain's share of world manufacturing production declined from 32% in 1870 to 15% in 1910 compared with a 100% increase in overseas British investment from two million pounds in 1900 to four million pounds in 1914. As he concludes about the British, "At the very moment when creativity and capital were needed for industrial renewal at home, resources were being siphoned away."[92] Even as these trends were emerging, Professor Aaron Friedberg points out that between 1870 and 1900, British GDP rose from 1.3 billion to 2.1 billion pounds and per capita national income rose from 29.9 to 42.5 pounds. Increases in absolute terms failed to halt Britain's relative decline as Friedberg adds, "The economic picture was not uniformly bleak, but what is apparent in retrospect is that in one critical area of

25

production after another Britain was being displaced by other countries...”[93] In relating

these circumstances to military power and of importance to the current U.S. situation,

Professor Paul Kennedy asserts, “...the fact remains that all of the major shifts in the

world’s *military-power* balances have followed alterations in the *productive*

balances...”[94]

A second lesson understood for a nation’s great power status is how it responds

to growing political and military challenges to its power within the international system,

given its own economic and fiscal situation. Habsburg Spain of the late 16th and early

17th centuries was facing multiple rising powers across the global environment.

Continental powers England, France, the Netherlands, and later Sweden and the north

German states (during the Thirty Years War) all were challenging Habsburg dominance

in Europe. England and the Dutch were contesting Spanish power and trade in its

overseas colonies and the Ottoman Turks were challenging Spain in southern Europe

and the Mediterranean Sea.[95] Spain had two grand strategic choices: first, contest all

of these challangers militarily coupled with a bid for economic self-sufficiency internal to

its empire, with a resulting increase in military expenditures and taxes in order to

maintain its hegemony; or, second, pursue a course of accommodation and cooperation

with these rising powers that included fiscal restraint, lower tariff and tax rates, and

improved trade to promote economic growth, and entailed military retrenchment that

maintained Spanish power, but not hegemony.[96] Spain chose the first course in order to

maintain its hegemony, but the constant wars and conflict across Europe and in the

New World depleted its treasury and negatively impacted the long-term prospects of the

Spanish economy.   Kennedy points out, “Between the mid-1500’s and 1630, there was a 500% increase in food prices and a 300% increase in industrial prices." Even an increase in military forces from 150K to 300K did not guarantee battlefield success for the Spanish.[97] As noted above, the empire defaulted multiple times on its debt and inflation was rampant. During this time, Spain also lost its technological lead in shipbuilding to the Dutch, textiles to the English, and metallurgy to the French and English.[98]

The overall impact was predictable as Lobell states, "...by the 17th century, virtually every sector of Spain's industry was depressed, and Spain was growing increasingly backward in the key growth industries of textiles, metallurgy, and shipbuilding, " and it had become dependent on foreign based industry and agriculture to meet its needs. By the 1640's Spain could no longer field a modern army or navy.[99] By the early 18th century, Spain was a second-rate power having lost its wars and lost its possessions in Flanders, central Europe, Italy, Portugal, and numerous overseas colonies in addition to ceding global leadership to England, France, and the Netherlands.[100] The lesson for the U.S. is that trying to pursue a similar grand strategy, which attempts to maintain U.S. hegemony or some type of policy close to it in terms of global predominance as the nation has enjoyed over the last sixty years, will seriously erode U.S. capabilities for the future across all elements of national power. Pursuing hegemony or global predominance to meet its stated national security goals is neither feasible nor acceptable given the nation's current finances. As Kennedy reminds, "At the center of the Spanish decline...was the failure to recognize the importance of preserving the economic underpinnings of a powerful military machine."[101]

Similarly, can the U.S. learn any lessons from the experiences of the British Empire? Like Habsburg Spain, the British Empire of the late 1800's and early 1900's was a global hegemon, resembling the current U.S. position in certain ways. As Kennedy explains about the British Empire, "...its combination of financial resources, productive capacity, imperial possessions, and naval strength meant that it was still probably the 'number one' world power, even if its lead was much less marked than in 1850."[102] Murray adds about the British situation,

> ....the erosion of the European concert, the expansion of colonial competition, and the changing global balance of power presented British statesmen at the turn of the century with the challenge of preserving an empire that many believed to be increasingly imperiled with means that they feared were becoming progressively less adequate.[103]

The British were facing multiple challenges to its global leadership position from the United States, Japan, France, Germany, and Russia and from a declining economic position on which to counter these contenders as evidenced by an industrial productive growth rate of only 1.5% annually from the period 1875 to 1894, half of what it had been annually since 1815.[104] Kennedy adds the British Empire situation mirrors the current U.S. slowdown in productivity and decrease in competitiveness,

> It involved such complex issues as national character, generational differences, the social ethos, and the educational system as well as more specific economic reasons like low investment, out-of-date plant, bad labor relations, poor salesmanship, and the rest...The 'workshop of the world' was now in third place, not because it wasn't growing, but because others were growing faster.[105]

In response, the British enacted a security policy of accommodation and selective cooperation with the rising powers, seeking to devolve regional security in the Americas to the United States and in the Pacific to Japan while using a combination of cooperation and confrontation with the other major powers to secure global British interests. These policies, which included promoting free trade and trying to relax international tensions, freed resources for the British to apply to the most important areas of the empire, but were not entirely successful with regards to Germany as Murray states, "...successive British leaders made repeated efforts to avoid antagonizing Germany and to find some formula that would satisfy Berlin's mounting ambitions without sacrificing British interests."[106] After 1905, international circumstances dictated that Britain move to a containment policy of Germany, drawing militarily and politically closer to France and Russia, the main alliance partners who would confront Germany during the First World War.[107]

British grand strategy during this period was only partially successful: it provided for security of the empire and its resources, but failed to regenerate core British economic capabilities and to prevent an outbreak of war that left the empire in a severely weakened economic and fiscal condition. The lesson for the U..S. is in trying to pursue a similar grand strategy, which attempts to use accommodation and selective confrontation with rising powers and traditional allies alike, rests equally on maintaining credible economic and military capabilities that provide the nation freedom of action during crisis without fear of general war or threatening the national interest. As RAND analysts Paul Davis and Peter Wilson explain,

> The historical experience of the United Kingdom with the United States and Germany early in the 20th century is worthy of consideration...the UK tried the policy of accommodation....[it] worked with the U.S. but failed with Germany...Overdrawing historical analogies is always troublesome, but the failure of accommodation between the United Kingdom and Germany should give the 21st-century leaders of the United States and China pause.[108]

Given this admonition, the U.S. clearly wants to avoid being put in the position of the British Empire during the 1930's which resulted directly from the outcomes of that disastrous first war. That war cost the British the equivalent of $40 billion dollars and caused them to accumulate a national debt worth 136% of its GDP afterwards, and by the mid-1920's, interest payments accounted for 50% of the British budget.[109] During the 1930's, the British faced more challenges to their global leadership from the likes of Germany, Italy, Japan, and Russia, but were in no position to offer any credible deterrent to these totalitarian powers. The United States even confronted the British over free trading policies that challenged the commercial protectionism of the empire. British industrial and financial strength was further weakened by the Great Depression, which forced cuts in military spending and necessitated a policy of appeasement to keep the peace and protect the empire.[110] Thus, British grand strategy of the 1930's was grounded in three assumptions: first, financial security overrode all other concerns even defense spending; second, Britain confronted no external threat requiring a rethinking of its defense policies; and third, appeasement was an adequate solution because the Continental situation did not warrant another major conflict.[111] The emphasis on fiscal security was influenced heavily by the weak British economic position of the 1930's and the inability to provide sufficient resources for defense.

None of these assumptions proved correct and Britain fought the Second World War from a position of economic and military weakness, and even though it was on the winning side against Fascism, the British would lose their empire in the post-war world. The outcome was not only driven by the war itself, but by the financial concessions Britain had to make to the U.S. in order to gain necessary financial support. The U.S. had its eye on the post-war economic environment and included clauses in the Atlantic

Charter and the Lend-lease Act calling for elimination of nondiscriminatory trade barriers, directly aimed at changing the existing trading system and opening British colonial markets to the U.S.[112] The lesson for the U.S. today, based upon the experience of the latter British Empire, is that the nation must eschew economic and military weakness and avoid the resulting dependence upon other powers for financial and capital support. What happened to post-war Britain economically at the hands of the U.S. could potentially happen to the U.S. at the hands of China and other rising powers in the future. As to this possibility, Asia Bureau Chief for *Institutional Investor* Allen Cheng observes,

> Beijing isn't angling to supplant the U.S. as the dominant power of the global economy, at least not yet. But officials do want to accelerate a shift from the so-called Washington consensus, under which the Clinton and Bush administrations set the agenda for global trade and financial liberalization, to a multilateral arrangement in which China and other emerging economic powers have much greater influence.[113]

Phillips concludes that the experiences of the Spanish Habsburg and British Empires uncover three potential Achilles tendons of leading economic powers that must be avoided in order to maintain great power status: first, a financial preoccupation and rentier culture coupled with a nonchalance towards production, build-up of debt, and increasingly transnational loyalties, that by implication undermine national ones; second, an aging technology and industrial base that is susceptible to technology transfers, foreign scientific innovation and migration of key industries; and lastly, the ruination and debt brought on by great-power diplomatic and military over-reach that paradoxically lives off the accumulated power from a previous era.[114] Phillips specifically referenced Spain and Britain, but he certainly had in mind the current U.S. situation when formulating these comments.

Although not directly comparable in every area, the primary lesson learned from these past examples centers on how critical a nation's economic well-being can influence the military and political balance of power within the international system, no matter the country-specific economic system. The U.S. must address its debt, move to a more balanced, competitive economy with emphasis on development, manufacture, and services within the emerging technology fields, restore U.S. credibility to sustain our power, and move away from a primarily high-finance economy as part of a broader grand strategy. Professor James Kurth points out that the Britain of the late 19th-century could have accomplished industrial transformation which would have created new industries (chemicals, automobiles, electric lights) to supplement the old ones, but by the early 1900's leadership in these industries had been passed to either Germany or the U.S. British financial interests preferred old industries in new countries to new industries in the old country because financial returns were better; therefore talent followed suit with the cream of British human capital pursuing careers in financial services and the civil service and retreating from business and engineering.[115] Friedberg reaches similar conclusions about the British Empire when he states,

> By 1900 a return to primacy was clearly impossible...Still, more could have been done to preserve Britain's position and to prepare the country for what was to come. There would surely have been dangers involved in following such a course, not least among them the possibility of a public backlash against the increased effort required to sustain a global role. But there were dangers, too, in trying to continue to play the part of world power without being willing to pay for the privilege.[116]

Proposed Grand Strategy

What then should comprise U.S. "Grand Strategy" for the future timeframe 2015 to 2030? The primary premise supporting this intention remains paramount: for the U.S. to preserve its ability to function as a great power within the international system of the

32

2030 to 2040 timeframe, the nation must regenerate its economic strength and recapitalize select defense capabilities during the 2015 to 2030 period. Not doing so risks this nation's long-term global position and power into the mid-21st century. The following proposal for national economic "renewal" within a national security context provides a broad design to address the main argument of this paper and consists of three main components – one psychological, one conceptual, and one that outlines prospective ends, ways, and means. The psychological component serves as a motivational instrument for change during this timeframe and provides an overall attitude shift to enhance the transition to a adapted way of visioning the U.S. role in the future international system. Second, the conceptual component of this grand strategy serves as the foundational structure on which to build the specific ends, ways, and means of the nation's intention. Lastly, the psychological and conceptual components of the grand strategy, in combination, provide the overall framework in which to unify and employ the specific ends, ways, and means proposals of this grand strategic design.

The psychological component consists of three main positions. First, the U.S. is and will remain a great power, but it must address its economic and fiscal problems to remain globally competitive. As the *Comeback America Initiative* (CAI) report states,

> The truth is, if we don't put our nation's finances in order and address the huge structural deficits and mounting debt burdens that lie ahead, America's position in the world, the job security of American workers, and our overall standard of living at home will suffer over time. Ultimately, even our national security and domestic tranquility could be called into question. The U.S. is a great nation - arguably the greatest in the history of mankind. The concept of American exceptionalism is real. It is rooted in the way our nation was founded, the documents that are the foundation of our government, and, most importantly, the people who comprise America. The U.S. federal government is a republic...In fact, the U.S. is

33

the longest standing republic still in existence, but not of all time. The Roman Republic lasted for over 500 years; however, it ceased to exist over 2,000 years ago due, in part, to fiscal irresponsibility by the government.[117]

Hormats calls for a return to the basic attitude that provided the necessary actions to sustain the nation's military strength and secure its national interests when he states,

> ...looking back over this nation's more than two hundred years, one central, constant theme emerges: sound national finances have proved to be indispensable to the country's military strength. Without the former, it is difficult over an extended period of time to sustain the latter. Generations of leaders have come to realize that if a country chronically lives beyond its means or misallocates its financial resources, it risks eroding its economic base and jeopardizes its ability to fund its national security requirements.[118]

Along similar lines, former Deputy Treasury Secretary Roger Altman highlights the connection between economic rejuvenation and national security when he advocates restoring the intellectual strength and credibility of the Anglo-Saxon brand of market-based capitalism, which provided much of the U.S. influence and soft power in the international system, and that was undermined by the 2008 economic crisis.[119] The CAI report concludes,

> Our republic was created through one of the greatest political documents in the history of mankind - the U.S. Constitution. That document is based on certain timeless principles, including limited but effective government, individual liberty and opportunity, equal justice under a rule of law, fiscal responsibility and sustainability, and inter-generational equity...From a financial perspective, our nation's Founders believed in certain core values like prudence, thrift, limited debt, savings and stewardship. Unfortunately, the facts reveal that within the past several decades, our nation and many Americans have strayed from these principles and values, and as a result, our future is now at risk. We must return to these timeless principles and values if we want America to stay great, and for our collective future to be better than our past.[120]

While economic revitalization is paramount through the 2030 timeframe, the second position involves the underlying attitude with which the U.S. should conduct its national security policy during this same time period. The U.S. can no longer afford to function exclusively as the "Enforcer, Philanthropist, and Savior" of the global community, but must become more disciplined and begin to practice some restraint. Cronin asserts, "The United States can best pursue a protracted period of global order by resisting the temptation to solve all the world's problems. The United States must pursue a strategy characterized by, in a word, restraint. Restraint is not a strategy, but it can help the United States preserve its limited means to focus on essential commitments."[121] Cronin rightly points out that "restraint" can have unintended consequences, such that adversaries can perceive weakness, allies and friends can sense a lack of commitment, or that the U.S. is judged a failure.[122] In actuality, an attitude of restraint coupled with the restoration of the nation's economic vitality and staying engaged within the international system with the targeted application of all elements of national power, can forthrightly mitigate such consequences. In many ways the combination of these two psychological positions rekindles the memory and words of what was written in 1949 as a U.S. call to arms against the Communist threat, but may now serve an even more timely call to action in the nation's present circumstances,

> Essentially, our democracy also possesses a unique degree of unity….expressions of national consensus in our society are soundly and solidly based…..These capabilities within us constitute a great potential force in our international relations. The potential within us of bearing witness to the values by which we live holds promise for a dynamic manifestation to the rest of the world of the vitality of our system. The essential tolerance of our world outlook, our generous and constructive impulses, and the absence of covetousness in our international relations are assets of potentially enormous influence.[123]

The aim to restore U.S. credibility and national power capability through 2030 leads to the third psychological position. The long-term desire and goal is to realize U.S.-"primacy' within the international system that guarantees the nation its desired place within that global order. Primacy is not hegemony nor is it "empire" under another name. Primacy, as defined by Art, is having superior influence, being able to win more often than others do, and possessing the most influential position, but not getting everything the nation wants all the time or every time. As he further explains, "...to be stronger than any other single actor is not to be in a position of dictating to each of them. To be the most important actor is not to be all-powerful, only the most powerful."[124] Primacy is entirely consistent with our current national security policies and national heritage of leadership within the international system. The grand strategy through the 2030 timeframe must position the U.S. to shoulder that "primacy" role for the 2030 to 2040 time period to sustain the nation's great power status into the mid-21st century.

Secondly, the conceptual component of this grand strategy consists of five themes, which in combination form a central, conceptual foundation for the overall design. First, the Periclean strategy of Athens used versus Spartan during the initial years of the Peloponnesian War, adapted to the current competitive international environment, offers a theme relevant for U.S. policy-makers. Pericles exhorted his fellow Athenians, in confronting the Spartan alliance, to be patient, pay attention to the needs of the military, attempt no new conquests that would drain the treasury, and expose the city to no new hazards because such a plan was designed to conserve the staying power of the city over the long-term.[125] In similar fashion, the U.S. must conserve its strength, and rebuild and revitalize its economy in order to prepare for more dangerous threats, remain competitive, and capitalize on potential opportunities in the 2030 – 2040 timeframe. Unfortunately, the Athenians proved incapable of executing the plan as Thucydides explains,

> What they did was the very contrary, allowing private ambitions and private interests, in matters apparently quite foreign to the war, to lead them into projects unjust both to themselves and to their allies—projects whose success would only conduce to the honor and advantage of private persons, and whose failure entailed certain disaster on the country in the war.[126]

This notion proved Pericles correct when he said, "...I am more afraid of our own blunders than that of the enemy's devices."[127]

To succeed where the Athenians failed, the U.S. should employ, as the second theme, a "Modified Off-Shore Balancing" model to prioritize our global interests and arrange our national power capabilities in a manner that allows the nation to rebuild its economic strength, partner with friends and allies, and protect the U.S.'s primary national interests. Professor Stephen Walt explains,

> It follows that the United States should eschew its present fascination with nation building and counterinsurgency and return to a grand strategy...labeled offshore balancing. Offshore balancing seeks to maintain...a balance of power among the strong states of Eurasia and of the oil-rich Persian Gulf...Instead of seeking to dominate these regions directly...our first recourse should be to have local allies uphold the balance of power, out of their own self-interest. Rather than letting them free ride on us, we should free ride on them as much as we can, intervening with ground and air forces only when a single power threatens to dominate some critical region. For an *offshore balancer*, the greatest success lies in getting somebody else to handle some pesky problem, not in eagerly shouldering that burden oneself.[128]

For the purposes of this paper's grand strategy proposal, full "Off-Shore Balancing," as advocated by Walt, is not suitable or acceptable to achieve U.S. global objectives and entails some adjustments. These modifications to his design require a conscious U.S. commitment directly to the Mid-East and Asia-Pacific regions due to continued regional security concerns and economic considerations, while devolving security responsibilities in other global regions to local alliances and coalitions, backed by U.S., North Atlantic

Treaty Organization (NATO), and United Nations (UN) support. It represents a policy

choice similar to what the British enacted in the late 1880's and early 1900's –

accommodation and selective confrontation. Lobell declares,

> If the hegemon devolves regional hegemony to liberal powers, the leader will lower the costs of leadership without harming its economic base. By amassing these freed-up resources in its remaining commitments, the hegemon will strengthen its immediate war-making capacity without extracting additional funds, thereby protecting its military security.[129]

A "modified off-shore balancing" scheme allows the U.S. to continue influencing the

rules of the international system game while not harming its long-term fiscal health; in

current circumstances, this means revitalizing the nation's economic strength.

The third theme involves the U.S. embracing the principles of Sun Tzu as an

operating belief, across the full range of operations and for use of all national power

elements when necessary, that would support a combined "Modified Off-Shore

Balancing" and Periclean-type stratagem. As Cronin contends,

> In the face of prolonged uncertainty, the best posture is to remain committed to the goal of building a sustainable, American-led order. Americans need to think more like Sun Tzu, who advocated winning whole and without fighting, and less like Clausewitz, for whom war was a continuation of politics by other means. Strategy must trump technology.[130]

Embracing Sun Tzu means that U.S. leaders must think in more imaginative and

creative ways to shape the nation's security environment to the nation's benefit. Sun

Tzu adroitly explained, "...those skilled at making the enemy move do so by creating a

situation to which the enemy must conform...a skilled commander seeks victory from

the situation..."[131] He added that the best policy is to attack the adversary's strategy

and then to disrupt his alliances.[132] Both statements support the judicious use of the

nation's capabilities in the execution of this grand strategy. The application of diplomatic, informational, military, and economic (DIME) force capabilities within each

component of this framework, based upon the specific situation, follows Sun Tzu's

concept of the normal and extraordinary forces. Sun Tzu described, "....use the normal

force to engage; use the extraordinary force to win....In battle there are only the normal

and extraordinary forces, but their combinations are limitless; none can comprehend

them all."[133] At any one time in execution of the strategy, three components of DIME

would constitute the normal force while the fourth would comprise the extraordinary

force. Sun Tzu was correct; the varying combinations of American DIME capabilities to

achieve the political and military objectives in this way would be limitless. Henry

Kissinger adds, "What distinguishes Sun Tzu from Western writers on strategy is the

emphasis on the psychological and political dimensions over the purely military...[he]

addresses the means of building a dominant political and psychological position, such

that the outcome of a conflict becomes a foregone conclusion."[134] Given the importance

of the mental aspect to the nation's grand strategy, adoption by leaders of the

"Maneuverist Approach" at all levels to support this embrace of Sun Tzu offers a mental

model to best manage diplomacy, power, and the use of capabilities against a thinking

adversary or competitor to achieve policy objectives. The "Manueverist Approach" is

defined as: "one in which shattering the enemy's overall cohesion and will to fight...is

paramount...Significant features are momentum and tempo, which in combination lead

to shock action and surprise...It calls for an attitude of mind in which doing the

unexpected and seeking originality is combined with a ruthless determination to

succeed."[135] At the grand strategic level, the "Manueverist Approach" embodies out-

thinking and out-witting our potential adversaries, both state and non-state actors, within the international system as necessary to secure our objectives. In a contest of "wills," this leadership model for using capabilities against an opponent or peer competitor is very much in the tradition of Sun Tzu, who stated, "....the general who understands war is the Minister of the people's fate and arbiter of the nation's destiny...One able to gain victory by modifying his tactics in accordance with the enemy situation may be said to be divine."[136] The nation's current situation certainly begs for political, economic and military leaders who, through the implementation of this grand strategy, can earn the *figurative* distinction of meeting Sun Tzu's definition of "divine."

The fourth conceptual component builds upon U.S. adoption of Sun Tzu's operating beliefs and involves establishing the theme of "dislocation" as the mechanism of first-choice in seeking a competitive strategic advantage over the nation's peer competitors and potential adversaries. As an operational and tactical concept, dislocation is defined as the "art of rendering the enemy's strength irrelevant. Through dislocation, the friendly force temporarily sets aside the enemy's advantage... and causes those strengths to be unrelated to the outcome of the conflict.[137] Taken to the grand strategic level, dislocation seeks to gain a position of advantage, when required within the international system, by rendering an opponent's strengths irrelevant and throwing his overall physical and psychological equilibrium as a great power off-balance, thus leaving that nation more agreeable to U.S. aims. This position of advantage is gained through the application of DIME capabilities in combination as described above; dislocation as a theme forms the basis of what Hart termed his "indirect approach" to winning by seeking advantage against the adversaries weak points and avoiding his strengths.[138] Given the need to preserve U.S. power and national capacities through the 2030 timeframe, the use of "dislocation" provides a conceptual focus for the overall acquisition and application of DIME capabilities throughout specific regions to secure the nation's interests.

The fifth and final theme involves essentially a "no penetration line" with regards to U.S. grand strategy and the ability to protect American national interests. As stated, the nation must recapitalize and regenerate its economic capabilities over the next 15 to 20 years in order to prepare for the challenges of the mid-21st century, and hence adjust its shorter term grand strategy to realize this aim. However, no potential adversary or peer competitor should mistake these actions as a sign of weakness in the nation's resolve during this transition period and the U.S. will resort to doing whatever is necessary to protect the security of the American people. America will not back down from confrontation if the situation requires that action. The U.S. is not withdrawing from the world community, it is going to make itself better. While it does so, potential adversaries would be wise not to challenge U.S. resolve in preserving and enhancing the current international system.

Lastly, the combined psychological and conceptual components of the grand strategy provide the overall framework in which to unify and employ the specific ends, ways, and means proposals of this grand strategic design. The first step involves establishing a prioritization of existing national objectives from the 2010 National Security Strategy, utilizing the framework advanced by Art. Priority of effort at this level is needed in order to focus the nation's limited resources on recapitalization and revitalization activities. The twin objectives of security for the U.S. and promoting economic growth for the nation clearly reach the level of "Vital," meaning these interests are designated as essential objectives that if not achieved will bring costs that are catastrophic to the U.S. or nearly so. The other two enduring objectives of values promotion and advancement of an international order, for the purposes of priority of strategic effort during the 2015 – 2030 timeframe, are designated as "Highly Important," meaning that if achieved bring great benefits to the nation, and if denied, carry severe costs but are not catastrophic in the long-term. The nation will still pursue these objectives within the revised prioritization scheme. In the economic and political domains, this grand strategy demands returning the nation to its historic roots with that focus on the nation's "Vital" interests. In advocating a solution to the nation's current situation, Hormats points out that,

> ...to manage the Cold War financial challenge...presidents Truman and Eisenhower reached deep into America's history, following George Washington's imperative that policy should serve the needs not only of the current generation but also of future generations and Alexander Hamilton's principle that sound national finances are a prerequisite for sustaining the country's military strength and security[139]

The nation's leaders must now enact policies commensurate with these roots and revised priorities. Economic growth and competitiveness is the key component as Kennedy asserts that the U.S. must balance security needs, provide for its citizens, and ensure sustained growth for the future,

> ...yet achieving the first feats—or either one of them—without the third will inevitably lead to relative eclipse over the longer term, which has of course been the fate of all slower-growing societies that failed to adjust to the dynamics of world power...It is hard to imagine, but a country whose productivity growth lags one(1) percent behind other countries over one century can turn, as England did, from the world's undisputed industrial leader into the mediocre economy it is today [1987]."[140]

Short-term tensions will invariably exist between funding for security, domestic, and economic programs. Hormats implores the nation's leaders to forestall that clash,

"Avoiding a clash requires reprioritization of budget policy, including cuts in non-essential spending in all budget categories, reforms in entitlement programs to ensure their sustainability, sufficient tax revenue to cover anticipated expenses, and room in the budget to meet emergencies."[141] The following constitutes the specific actions the U.S. must take to regenerate its economic and political vitality:

- Reform the federal tax code and adjust tax rates to ensure that sufficient revenues are available to resource achievement of primarily the two "Vital" national objectives, most especially economic revitalization, and then secondarily, the two "Highly Important" national interests. These efforts should provide revenues at the 20 to 21% of GDP target level during the duration of this grand strategy.

- Reform existing entitlement programs to ensure the long-term health of these programs and reduce in real terms their increasing share of both the federal budget and GDP. Ensure these social welfare reforms provide for the most vulnerable of the nation's citizens as priority, and that "...those who can pay more for, or whose financial circumstances enable them to rely less on these programs, should be called upon to do so."[142]

- Reduce the growth of federal spending and reallocate revenues to the highest priority ventures and away from low-priority programs. These efforts should reduce the federal budget's share of GDP to historical levels of 18 to 19%, with the aim of bringing the federal budget into balance during the timeframe of this grand strategy. In addition, establish an interim target of reducing the debt-to-GDP ratio to 60% and then finally to the historical U.S. average of 40%.[143] These actions establish the conditions to begin reducing the nation's long-term debt and annual interest payments, and increase annual GDP growth into the 2030 to 2040 time period.

- Create a public/private infrastructure funding mechanism, such as a government-sponsored infrastructure bank, to provide necessary resource streams to fund the recapitalization of the nation's infrastructure across all required spheres that will stimulate economic activity.[144] These efforts should increase the nation's annual spending on infrastructure to 4 to 5% of GDP with an estimated increase in that GDP of $1.59 for every infrastructure dollar spent.[145] In addition, this effort would include revitalizing the nation's secondary and higher education systems in order to educate and train a U.S. workforce able to successfully compete in the mid-21st century.

- Reform and consolidate the existing structure of the federal government, to include sensible reductions in the size of the federal workforce, and streamlining and consolidating departments in order to conserve resources. Consolidating the increasingly related departments of labor, commerce and education, for example, would result in a department of around 67,000 employees with less overhead staffing and that would still be only the 10th largest cabinet and agency-level entity.[146]

- Reduce the complexity of regulations in order to enhance overall economic growth and corresponding employment. Establish conditions at the federal level that enhance the private's sector ability to develop and exploit emerging technologies, to include exploring all available energy alternatives to reduce our dependence on foreign oil and increase national R&D spending, and translate those improvements into a rejuvenated manufacturing and service sector that provides for a more balanced, expanding national economy.

- Reform or establish the required executive and legislative branch processes, actions and activities to streamline execution and oversight of this grand strategy.

This program is not dissimilar to the one proposed within the 1950 National Security Council Memorandum 68 (NSC-68). The threat then was the Soviet Union; the threat now, requiring an equally comprehensive response, is the nation's long-term economic health and managing its position within the international system.[147] As Walt declares,

> And so, the biggest challenge the United States faces today is not a looming great-power rival; it is the triple whammy of accumulated debt, eroding infrastructure and a sluggish economy. The only way to have the world's most capable military forces both now and into the future is to have the world's most advanced economy, and that means having better schools, the best universities, a scientific establishment that is second to none, and a national infrastructure that enhances productivity and dazzles those who visit from abroad. These things all cost money, of course, but they would do far more to safeguard our long-term security than spending a lot of blood and treasure determining who should run Afghanistan, Kosovo, South Sudan, Libya, Yemen or any number of other strategic backwaters...Instead of building new Bagrams in faraway places of little consequence, it is time to devote more attention to that "shining city on a hill" of which our leaders often speak, but which still remains to be built.[148]

While the primary and essential emphasis of this design is on revitalizing our economic strength and competitiveness, the U.S. must still provide global leadership and look to its security needs within the international system. The nation will have fewer resources than in the past for this endeavor. The U.S. must therefore prioritize requirements in pursuing this paper's definition of its "Vital" national security objective, leveraging the themes outlined above under the conceptual component of this grand strategy. During the 2015 – 2030 timeframe, therefore, the U.S. global security focus will center on the Mid-East and Asia-Pacific regions while devolving designated security responsibilities in other global regions to local area alliances, bi-lateral and multi-lateral coalitions, and our traditional allies and partners. The U.S. will provide security assistance and increased diplomatic support, in partnership with friends, allies, and non-governmental actors, to realize this goal. U.S. will recapitalize and prioritize military power capabilities for employment in these two critical regions while other forms of national power represent the mechanisms of first-choice to support regional security arrangements in other parts of the world. The U.S. must pursue the following actions within the military and diplomatic domains in order to successfully execute the grand strategic design:

- Create and execute innovative diplomatic and security cooperation processes that maximize the nation's flexibility in rapidly forming coalitions and alliances to ensure regional security and respond to crisis in the *non-priority* regions of the globe. Support and leverage NATO, the most successful military and political alliance in history, and both our traditional and non-traditional partners to realize this capability. Macdonald and Parent point out, "Holding on to exposed and expensive commitments simply for the sake of one's reputation is a greater geopolitical gamble than withdrawing to cheaper, more defensible frontiers…and will help alleviate an unsustainable financial position."[149]

- Likewise, prioritize diplomatic, economic and security cooperation capabilities and efforts with our allies in the Mid-East and Asia-Pacific regions that foster attainment of our national interests as well as those of our regional partners and friends. Professor Joseph Nye explains, "An increasing number of challenges will require the United States to exercise power with others as much as power over others…The country's capacity to maintain alliances and create networks will be an important dimension of its hard and soft power."[150]

45

- Within a whole-of-government approach, develop capabilities and processes to apply coercive economic diplomacy and statecraft measures that compliment and/or supplement the traditional forms of national power to affect our national security goals. These activities will focus on financial, economic, and business model vulnerabilities of the nation's adversaries, involving both state and non-state actors. Strategic analyst David Asher asserts, "…because of the high degree of economic globalization and expanded economic and financial ties between countries, economic, financial and legal means are likely to be used more frequently in the years ahead."[151]

- As priority defense effort, modernize and recapitalize within budgetary resource constraints appropriate ISR, space, cyber, air, nuclear, naval, knowledge systems, and special operating force capabilities that provide the nation continued access to the global commons and allow the nation to pursue its revised defense strategy. This modernization effort will provide the nation sufficient force levels, which include forward deployed forces, to implement regional security and contingency plans within the prioritized regions, and allow the nation to pursue global strategies to combat transnational, extremist, and WMD threats from both state and non-state actors.

- Maintain and employ an effective national and defense intelligence force capability to ensure the nation's leaders receive adequate and timely information on which to avoid strategic surprise, make informed decisions, and employ required capabilities. As Sun Tzu stated, "And therefore only the enlightened sovereign and the worthy general who are able to use the most intelligent people as agents are certain to achieve great things. Secret operations are essential in war; upon them the army relies to make its every move."[152]

- Reshape and realign our ground and marine force capabilities to ensure the necessary force projection capabilities are retained and modernized to implement the nation's regional security and contingency plans within the prioritized regions. For ground, marine, and other force capabilities the nation simply cannot afford during this timeframe, realign them to the reserve component as a 'strategic' hedge in the event of an unforeseen crisis or contingency operation. In addition, reshape and revisit the nation's homeland defense and homeland security capabilities to ensure only the most critical and vital components are prioritized for funding during this timeframe as a method to conserve resources.

Implementation of the provisions of this grand strategy for the 2015 – 2030 will establish the necessary conditions for the U.S. to maintain its great power status into the 2030 – 2040 timeframe. Cronin observes,

> The preservation of American power, rather than the full and short-term exertion of it, may be most beneficial to preserving future global stability…The United States can reform its institutions, rebalance its books and invest in its people, while simultaneously pursuing more effective alliances and partnerships. Getting America's own house in order is equally important and well within the capacity of mature leaders who exhibit foresight and strategic restraint. If legitimacy buttresses power, and indeed can be tantamount to power, then the United States needs to "learn to conduct its foreign policy with greater wisdom and restraint." The need for effective American leadership in international affairs remains undiminished.[153]

Conclusion

America is a great country and will remain a great power if it chooses to pursue the necessary actions to rebuild its economic strength and competitiveness as proposed in this paper and grand strategy. As far back as 1987, Paul Kennedy implored the U.S. to pursue a reasonable balance between security ends and means, and preserve the technological and economic basis of its power from relative erosion.[154] Over the last 25 years, that call went unheeded and now the nation finds itself in a difficult position. The CAI report observes,

> America is at a critical crossroads and the choices that our elected officials make, or fail to make, over the next five years will largely determine whether our future is brighter than our past. We must return to the time tested principles and values that made us a great nation. Yes, we can return to those principles and values while making the tough choices necessary to put our finances in order in a reasoned and reasonable manner to keep America great and the American Dream alive. However, to be successful, the first three words in the Constitution must come alive - "We the People". We the People are ultimately responsible and accountable for what does or does not happen in Washington, as well as in our state capitals and city halls.[155]

A call to the American people is not new. Within NSC-68, the document's authors knew that to confront the threat from the Soviet Union, the American people would be called

upon to bear the financial burdens of a U.S. military build-up. The memorandum states,

> But there are risks in making ourselves strong. A large measure of
> sacrifice and discipline will be demanded of the American people. They
> will be asked to give up some of the benefits which they have come to
> associate with their freedoms.....Our fundamental purpose is more likely
> to be defeated from lack of the will to maintain it, than from any mistakes
> we may make....No people in history have preserved their freedom who
> thought that by not doing enough to protect themselves they might prove
> inoffensive to their enemies.[156]

62 years later, the American people again are called upon to sacrifice and maintain their

nation's freedom, strength and power, this time from the threat of internal economic

ruin. Critics of this grand strategy proposal will invariably point out that any retreat from

the current U.S. position within the global order will spell long-term national doom,

sacrificing the security efforts of the last 60 years; they contend the U.S. is not in any

type of decline and should not act like it is. Emblematic of this viewpoint is Historian

Robert Kagan who wrote recently in *The New Republic* challenging any "declinist"

viewpoints, essentially stating that the U.S. has as much global power and influence

today than it has ever had. In terms of the U.S. economic situation he states,

> Perhaps the greatest concern underlying the declinist mood...is not really
> whether the United States can afford to continue playing its role in the
> world. It is whether Americans are capable of solving any of their most
> pressing economic and social problems. As many statesmen and
> commentators have asked, can Americans do what needs to be done to
> compete effectively in the twenty-first century world?[157]

Kagan answers his own question is saying, "Who Knows?," and then proceeds to

explain that because the U.S. has overcome adversity in the past, we may well likely

overcome it again; not really the stuff of which effective and durable grand strategies

are made and not consistent with the grand strategy proposal explained in this paper.

Staunch opponents of the "declinist" view may well be reminded of what Friedberg observed of Britain when he stated, "In 1900 most Englishmen probably still shared an overarching confidence in the superiority of their own country, which as time passed, was based more on faith and habit than on facts."[158] In an updated version of this same notion before a 2003 speech to the U.S. Congress, Prime Minister Tony Blair stated, "All predominant power seems for a time invincible, but in fact, it is transient." Niall Ferguson therefore inquires, "The question Americans must ask themselves is just how transient they wish their predominance to be. Though the barbarians have already knocked at the gates—once spectacularly— imperial decline in this case seems more likely to come, as it came to Gibbon's Rome, from within."[159] Relevant to the main argument of this paper and its associated grand strategy proposal that wholly seeks to mitigate that internal U.S. decline, Liam Fox concludes, "To be a hawk on defence, you need to be a hawk on the deficit and the national debt too...The bottom line is that a strong economy is a national security requirement...There are no easy answers. There are no silver bullets. There are only tough decisions, hard work and perseverance. To pretend otherwise is to fail in our duty to our country and its people."[160]

Endnotes

[1] Richard N. Haass, "The Restoration Doctrine," *The American Interest*, Winter (January/February) 2012, 50.

[2] B. H. Liddell Hart, *Strategy – 2nd Revised Edition*, (New York, NY: Meridian Printing, Penguin Group, 1991), 359.

[3] C. Fred Bergsten, "The Dollar and Deficits," *Foreign Affairs*, November/December 2009, in ProQuest (accessed November 12, 2011).

[4] Patrick M. Cronin, *Restraint – Recalibrating American Strategy*, (Washington, DC: Center for a New American Security, June 2010), 5.

[5] For the purposes of this paper, the term hegemon is defined as "the situation where one individual nation-state has the sole power to establish and maintain the essential rules governing inter-state relations within the international system, and is willing to use its power to do so." For a detailed analysis of whether the United States constitutes an empire or a hegemon, which is beyond the scope of this paper, see Charles-Philippe David and David Grondin, *Hegemony or Empire? – The Redefinition of US Power under George W. Bush*, (Aldershot, UK: Ashgate Publishing Limited, 2006).

[6] Haass, 50.

[7] Fareed Zakaria, "The Future of American Power: How America Can Survive the Rise of the Rest," *Foreign Affairs*, May/June 2008, in ProQuest, (accessed November 12, 2011).

[8] Paul K. MacDonald and Joseph M. Parent, "Graceful Decline? The Surprising Success of Great Power Retrenchment," *International Security*, Spring 2011, 22.

[9] Steven E. Lobell, *The Challenge of Hegemony – Grand Strategy, Trade, and Domestic Politics*, (Ann Arbor, MI: University of Michigan Press, 2003), 3.

[10] Ibid., 3.

[11] Ibid., 40.

[12] Robert J. Art, *A Grand Strategy for America*, (Ithaca, NY: Century Foundation, Cornell University Press, 2003), 81.

[13] John J. Mearsheimer, *Liddell Hart and the Weight of History*, (London, UK: Brassey's Defence Publishers, 1988), 17.

[14] Ibid., 17. Lobell also supports the view that grand strategy has fiscal and political aspects in addition to the traditional military ones, and secondly, grand strategy does not end or begin with wars, but spans peacetime as well. See Lobell's *The Challenge of Hegemony – Grand Strategy, Trade, and Domestic Politics*, 3.

[15] Hart, 322.

[16] Williamson Murray and Richard Hart Seinreich, *The Shaping of Grand Strategy – Policy, Diplomacy, and War*, (Cambridge, UK: Cambridge University Press, 2011), 2-3 and 8.

[17] Daniel Drezner, "Does Obama Have a Grand Strategy? – Why We Need Doctrines in Uncertain Times," *Foreign Affairs,* in ProQuest, (accessed January 15, 2012).

[18] Ibid.

[19] Murray and Seinreich, 32-33.

[20] Art, 3.

[21] National Intelligence Council (NIC), *Global Trends 2025 – A Transformed World*, (Washington, DC: Office of the Director of National Intelligence, November 2008), vi.

[22] United States Joint Forces Command (USJFCOM), "The Joint Operating Environment 2010," http://www.peakoil.net/files/JOE2010.pdf. (accessed November, 20, 2011), 10.

[23] NIC, vi.

[24] Ibid., vii.

[25] Cronin, 13. Additionally, the Winter 2012 version of the *T. Rowe Price Investment Report* points out many clear advantages that developing markets as a whole currently possess over the developed world: economic growth that is 4% greater, higher consumer demand and capital spending, and higher corporate profitability. The BRIC nations specifically are experiencing increases in annual incomes among working and middle-income families, leading to increased purchasing power.

[26] NIC, vii.

[27] Arvind Subramanian, "The Inevitable Superpower: Why China's Dominance Is a Sure Thing," *Foreign Affairs*, September/October 2011, in ProQuest, (accessed November 15, 2011).

[28] Michael Beckley, "China's Century? – Why America's Edge Will Endure," *International Security*, Winter 2011/12, 43 and 77.

[29] Haass, 51.

[30] Roger Altman, "The Great Crash, 2008: A Geopolitical Setback for the West," *Foreign Affairs*, January/February 2009, in ProQuest, (accessed November 15, 2011).

[31] Stephen M. Walt, "The End of the American Era," *The National Interest*, November/December 2011, 12.

[32] NIC, 94 and 97.

[33] Ibid., 46 and 47.

[34] Ibid., viii-ix.

[35] USJFCOM, 57.

[36] Neyla Arnas, *Fighting Chance – Global Trends and Shocks in the National Security Environment,* (Washington, DC: National Defense University Press and Potomac Books, Inc. 2009), 2.

[37] NIC, 71.

[38] Ibid., 71.

[39] USJFCOM, 34.

[40] NIC, x.

[41] President Barak Obama, "United States National Security Strategy – May 2010", White House, http://www.whitehouse.gov/sites/default/files/rss_viewer/national_security_strategy.pdf (accessed December 15, 2011), 7 and 17.

[42] Michael Mandelbaum, *The Frugal Superpower – America's Global Leadership in a Cash-Strapped Era*, (New York, NY: Public Affairs, 2010), 45.

[43] Cronin, 7 and 10.

[44] Ibid., 5.

[45] Lieutenant General David W. Barno, USA (Ret), Nora Bensahel and Travis Sharp, "Hard Choices – Responsible Defense in an Age of Austerity,(Washington, DC: Center for a New American Security, October 2011), 5.

[46] Art, 45.

[47] Ibid., 45.

[48] MacDonald and Parent, "Graceful Decline?", 19.

[49] Right Honorable Doctor Liam Fox, MP, UK Secretary of State for Defence, "Transcript – Strong Economy, Strong Defence, Strategic Reach: Protecting National Security in the 21st Century," *Chatham House*, http://www.chathamhouse.org/publications/papers/view/1712254, (accessed December 15, 2011), 4.

[50] Klaus Schwab, Editor, *Global Competitiveness Report 2010-11*, (Geneva, Switzerland: World Economic Forum, 2010), 4.

[51] Ibid., 14.

[52] Ibid., 4-9. These pages give an individual, detailed description of the twelve pillars.

[53] Ibid., 16. "Efficiency Enhancers" include the pillars of higher education and training, goods market efficiency, labor market efficiency, financial market development, technological readiness, and market size. "Innovation and Sophistication Factors" include the pillars of business sophistication and innovation.

[54] Ibid., 4. By way of comparison with certain allies and economic competitors in this basic category, the rankings were as follows: Brazil (86th), India (81st), China (30th), UK (18th), France (16th), Australia (12th), Canada (11th), and Germany (6th).

[55] Ibid., 4.

[56] NIC, 8.

[57] Gautam Naik, "R&D Spending to Keep on Climbing," *Wall Street Journal,* Friday, December 16, 2011, A4.

[58] Schwab, 4.

[59] American Society of Civil Engineers, "2009 Report Card for America's Infrastructure," http://www.infrastructurereportcard.org (accessed October 27, 2011), 3-7.

[60] Mark Gerenscer, "Re-imagining Infrastructure," *The American Interest*, March/April 2011, 35.

[61] William Galston, "Bank On It: A Conversation with Bernard Schwartz," *The American Interest*, March/April 2011, 47.

[62] Schwab, 5.

[63] Sean Kay, *Global Security in the 21st Century – The Quest for Power and the Search for Peace*, (Lanham, MD: Rowman and Littlefield, INC., 2006), 354-355.

[64] Schwab, 5.

[65] *Trading Economics*, "United States Government Debt To GDP," http://www.tradingeconomics.com/united-states/government-debt-to-gdp (Accessed December 20, 20011).

[66] Comeback America Initiative (CAI), "Comeback America: Restoring Fiscal Sanity," http://www.tcaii.org/UploadedFiles/072011%20Restoring%20Fiscal%20Sanity%20Washington%20DC.pdf, 4.

[67] Paul K. MacDonald and Joseph M. Parent, "The Wisdom of Retrenchment: America Must Cut Back to Move Forward," *Foreign Affairs*, November/December 2011, (accessed December 12, 2011).

[68] Bergsten, in ProQuest.

[69] Anthony H. Cordesman, "Rethinking a Resource-Based Strategy," (Washington, DC: Center for Strategic and International Studies, February 28, 2011), 8.

[70] Robert D. Hormats, *The Price of Liberty – Paying for America's Wars from the Revolution to the War on Terror*, (New York, NY: Times Books, Henry Holt and Company, 2007), 288.

[71] Frank A. DiStasio, Jr., *Army Budget – An Analysis Fiscal Year 2012*, (Arlington, VA: Association of the United States Army, 2011), 5.

[72] Hormats, 288.

[73] MacKenzie Eaglen, "U.S. Defense Spending: The Mismatch Between Plans and Resources, " *Heritage Foundation*, June 7, 2010, http://thf_media.s3.amazonaws.com/2010/pdf/bg2418.pdf (Accessed February 2, 2012).

[74] *Trading Economics*, "United States GDP Annual Growth Rate," http://www.tradingeconomics.com/united-states/gdp-growth-annual (Accessed December 20, 2011).

[75] World Bank – Economic Data Indicators, "Annual % GDP Growth Table," http://data.worldbank.org/indicator/NY.GDP.MKTP.KD.ZG/countries?display=default (Accessed January 26, 2012). From 2001 to 2010, by way of comparison, China's GDP growth rate never fell below 8.3%, and exceeded 10% during six years of the decade, respectively (2003-2007, and 2010).

[76] DiStasio, 13.

[77] Hormats, 283.

[78] CAI, 3. Duties of the Comptroller General, which includes evaluating and reporting on Executive Branch programs and the use of federal funds, are described in U.S. Code Title 15, Chapter 16B, Subchapter 1, Paragraph 771.

[79] Iwan Morgan, "The Indebted Empire: America's Current-Account Deficit Problem," *International Politics*, January 2008, 96-97. The first part of Morgan's assertion actually comes from Sherle R. Schwenninger's article entitled "America's Suez Moment,' in the January/February 2004 edition of *The Atlantic Monthly*.

[80] Zakaria, in ProQuest.

[81] Niall Ferguson, *Colossus – The Price of America's Empire*, (New York, NY: Penguin Press, 2004), 262.

[82] Hormats, xxi.

[83] Daniel Drezner, "Bad Debts: Assessing China's Financial Influence in Great Power Politics," *International Security*, Fall 2009, 34.

[84] Ibid., 13 and 16.

[85] Ferguson, 262 and 269.

[86] Schwab, 23.

[87] David M. Walker, "We the People: Keeping the Economy and the Nation Strong," *Economic Security – Neglected Dimension of National Security?*, (Washington, DC: National Defense University Press, 2011), 12.

[88] Ferguson, 279.

[89] USJFCOM, 22.

[90] Henry Kissinger, *On China*, (New York, NY: Penguin Press, 2011), 522.

[91] Kevin Phillips, *Wealth and Democracy*, (New York, NY: Broadway Books, 2002), 174 & 178.

[92] Ibid., 185-186.

[93] Aaron L. Friedberg, *The Weary Titan: Britain and the Experience of Relative Decline, 1895-1905*, (Princeton, NJ: Princeton University Press, 1988), 24-25.

[94] Paul Kennedy, *The Rise and Fall of the Great Powers – Economic Change and Military Conflict from 1500 to 2000*, (New York, NY: Random House, 1987), 439.

[95] Lobell, 123.

[96] Ibid., 124-131.

[97] Kennedy, 46.

[98] Lobell, 125-126.

[99] Ibid., 151.

[100] Ibid., 164.

[101] Kennedy, 55.

[102] Ibid., 231.

[103] Murray and Seinreich, 119.

[104] Kennedy, 227.

[105] Ibid., 228.

[106] Murray and Seinreich, 143.

[107] Lobell, 45 and 82-84.

[108] Paul K. Davis and Peter A. Wilson, Looming Discontinuities in U.S. Military Strategy and Defense Planning, (Arlington, VA: RAND Corporation National Defense Research Institute, 2011), 31.

[109] Zakaria, in ProQuest.

[110] Kennedy, 315-317.

[111] Murray and Seinreich, 150.

[112] Lobell, 121.

[113] Allen Cheng, "China Wants to Reshape the International Financial System," *Institutional Investor,* September 2009, in ProQuest (accessed November 15, 2011).

[114] Phillips, 197-200.

[115] James Kurth, "The Foreign Policy of Plutocracies," *The American Interest*, November/December 2011, 11.

[116] Friedberg, 303.

[117] CAI, 2.

[118] Hormats, xiii.

[119] Roger Altman, "The Great Crash, 2008: A Geopolitical Setback for the West," *Foreign Affairs*, January/February 2009, in ProQuest, (accessed November 12, 2011).

[120] CAI, 2.

[121] Cronin, 6.

[122] Ibid., 23.

[123] National Security Council Memorandum 68 (NSC-68), http://www.usnwc.edu/ NavalWarCollegeReviewArchives/1970s/1975%20May-June.pdf (accessed 19 December, 2011), 69.

[124] Art, 90.

[125] Robert B. Strassler, *The Landmark Thucydides – A Comprehensive Guide to the Peloponnesian War*, (New York, NY: Touchstone Books, Simon and Schuster, 1998), 127, paragraph 2.65.

[126] Ibid., 127, paragraph 2.65.

[127] Ibid., 83-84, paragraph 1.444.

[128] Stephen M. Walt, "The End of the American Era," *The National Interest*, November/December 2011, 13.

[129] Lobell, 41.

[130] Cronin, 25.

[131] Samuel B. Griffith, ed., *Sun Tzu – The Art of War*, (New York, NY: Oxford University Press, 1963), 93.

[132] Ibid., 77.

[133] Ibid., 91-92.

[134] Kissinger, 26.

[135] U.K. Ministry of Defence, *British Defence Doctrine*, Joint Warfighting Publication 0-01, (Shrivenham, UK: The Joint Doctrine & Concepts Centre, 2001), 3-5.

[136] Griffith, 76 and 101.

[137] Robert R. Leonhard, *The Principles of War for the Information Age*, (Novato, CA: Presidio Press, 1998), 64 - 65. Leonhard elaborates more on the concept of dislocation in two of his other books, *The Art of Maneuver* and *Fighting By Minutes: Time and the Art of War*. See also Richard E. Simpkin's *Race to the Swift: Thoughts on Twenty-First Century Warfare*, for a further explanation of the dislocation concept, pages 139-142.

[138] Hart, 5-6 and 325-326. See also Kissinger's *On China*, 23-25, for his discussion on the differences between Chinese and Western strategic theory and tradition as expressed by the most popular strategic games in each region, "Wei Qi" and "Chess," respectfully.

[139] Hormats, 280.

[140] Kennedy, 446.

[141] Hormats, 283.

[142] Ibid., 289.

[143] Donald B. Marron, "America in the Red," *National Affairs*, Spring 2010, 10-11.

[144] Galston, 49-50.

[145] Gerenscer, 45.

[146] Curtis W. Copeland, *The Federal Workforce: Characteristics and Trends*, (Washington, DC: Congressional Research Service, April 19, 2011), 6.

[147] NSC-68, 100-101. See also pages 105-106 which incorporates strategic policy recommendations from the earlier NSC Memo 20/4 written by George Kennan in 1948.

[148] Walt, 16.

[149] MacDonald and Parent, "Graceful Decline?", 41 and 43.

[150] Joseph S. Nye, Jr. "The Future of American Power: Dominance and Decline in Perspective," *Foreign Affairs*, November/December 2010, in ProQuest, (accessed November 12, 2011).

[151] Davis Asher, Victor Comras, and Patrick M. Cronin, *Pressure – Coercive Economic Statecraft and US National Security*, (Washington, DC: Center for a New American Security, January 2011), 15.

[152] Griffith, 149.

[153] Cronin, 25 and 30.

[154] Kennedy, 514.

[155] CAI, 37.

[156] NSC-68, 81.

[157] Robert Kagan, "Not Fade Away: Against the Myth of American Decline," *The New Republic,* February 2, 2012, 25.

[158] Friedberg, 282.

[159] Ferguson, 302. The spectacular event to which the author refers is the 9-11 attack.

[160] Fox, 6 and 11.

www.ingramcontent.com/pod-product-compliance
Lightning Source LLC
Chambersburg PA
CBHW080545290526
45790CB00006B/2559